TOP TENS

KILLER DINOSAURS

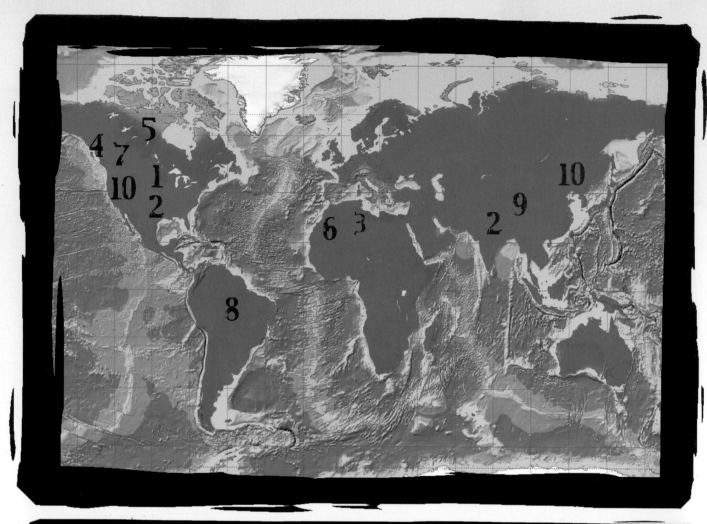

1 DEINONYCHUS	6 CARCHARODONTOSAURUS
2 TYRANNOSAURUS REX	7 TROODON
3 SPINOSAURUS	8 GIGANTOSAURUS
4 ALLOSAURUS	9 VELOCIRAPTOR
5 ALBERTOSAURUS	10 DILOPHOSAURUS

Copyright © ticktock Entertainment Ltd 2005
First published in Great Britain in 2005 by ticktock Media Ltd,
Unit 2, Orchard Business Centre, North Farm Road, Tunbridge Wells, Kent TN2 3XF
ISBN 1 86007 913 x pbk
Printed in China
A CIP catalogue record for this book is available from the British Library.

CONTENTS

The period of Earth's history between 245 and 65 million years ago is often known as the **Age of Dinosaurs**. There were thousands of different dinosaurs; most were peaceful herbivores, but some were ferocious, meat-eating predators. This book presents our Top Ten of the most dangerous dinosaurs, rated according to:

BODY MASS

Size was obviously important for a dinosaur predator. The bigger the predator, the bigger the prey it can attack. Similarly with weight, a heavy predator will find it easier to drag down and overpower its prey. We gave our dinosaurs a combined score based on their size and weight, but also taking into consideration the average size of their prey in each case.

Velociraptor lived in Asia towards the end of the **Cretaceous** period. The first remains of this dinosaur were discovered in Mongolia by Henry Osborn in 1924. Velociraptor had a winning combination of speed, aggression and fearsome weapons – only its small size prevents it from being the overall winner. It was the size of a small turkey!

BODY MASS
An average Velociraptor would have been about 1.5 metres long, and just a metre tall at the hip. This dinosaur would have weighed about 20-25 kilograms.

JAW POWER
It had about 80 teeth that were designed for ripping and tearing flesh. Narrow **jaws** allowed Velociraptor to push its head inside the **carcass** of a dinosaur.

MOBILITY
Velociraptor was a fast-running **bipedal** dinosaur, capable of reaching speeds of 40 mph. Its name means "speedy thief."

JAW POWER

Most dinosaur predators relied entirely on their jaws for killing, as well as eating. We based our score on the size and strength of the jaws, together with the number, length, and sharpness of the teeth. Only a few dinosaurs, such as our overall winner Deionychus, had claws that were also efficient weapons, and they were awarded bonus points.

MOBILITY

High speed gives a predator a tremendous advantage – but speed alone is not everything. There is no point in being able to run faster than your prey, if you cannot change direction easily, or come to a sudden stop. Our dinosaur predators were given points for their speed, acceleration, and agility; with extra points awarded to those with good jumping skills.

FRIGHT FACTOR

Meat-eating dinosaurs employed a wide variety of hunting techniques. Some were pack-hunters, while other lived and hunted alone. Some dinosaurs preferred to wait in ambush for their prey, while others were constantly on the prowl for something to eat. We based our scores on the overall efficiency of the technique that was most frequently employed.

HUNTING SKILLS

Some of the meat-eating dinosaurs were as big as a bus – and any predator that size is frightening. Exactly how frightening depends on how close you are. The closer you are, the less time you have to decide before you are eaten. The largest dinosaurs were not always the most frightening, however.

About 12 Velociraptor fossils have been found so far. One is thought to have died whilst fighting a Protoceratops.

Velociraptor (above right) was one of the fastest and fiercest predators that ever lived.

FRIGHT FACTOR

Velociraptor was not much larger than a pet cat, but you would not want to meet a pack of these vicious little dinosaurs.

HUNTING SKILLS

Velociraptor was a pack hunter and a highly efficient predator. It attacked with the claws of all four limbs, and could even jump up onto the back of its prey.

EXTREME SCORES

Too small to be more highly rated on an individual basis, but a pack of them would be a different matter.

MOBILITY 10/10

BODY MASS 1/10

JAW POWER 2/10

FRIGHT FACTOR 1/10

HUNTING SKILLS 8/10

= TOTAL SCORE

9

5

Dilophosaurus lived during the early part of the **Jurassic** period. This **carnivore** had a distinctive **crest** made from a double layer of bone along the top of its skull. This colourful strip would have been used for communication. The **fossil** remains of Dilophosaurus were discovered in 1942 in Arizona, USA, by the palaeontologist Samuel Welles.

Dilophosaurus had an unusually long tail for an active predator.

BODY MASS

Dilophosaurus was about six metres in length, and weighed about 500 kilograms. It had a slender build but was a ferocious fighter.

MOBILITY

Dilophosaurus was a **bipedal** animal that hunted by chasing its **prey**. Powerful muscles in the hind limbs enabled it to run quickly.

JAW POWER

Although Dilophosaurus' **jaw** were packed with long sharp teeth, they were fairly weak.

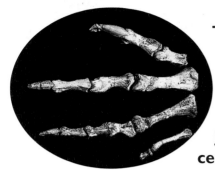

The claws at the ends of the fingers and toes were very sharp, but they were just a few centimetres long.

FRIGHT FACTOR

Dilophosaurus was big enough to look scary, but those jaws were not as strong as they looked. Its claws were deadly.

HUNTING SKILLS

Most scientists believe that Dilophosaurus hunted in packs, so it could attack animals much larger than itself. Some scientists, however, think that Dilophosaurus fed only on **carrion**.

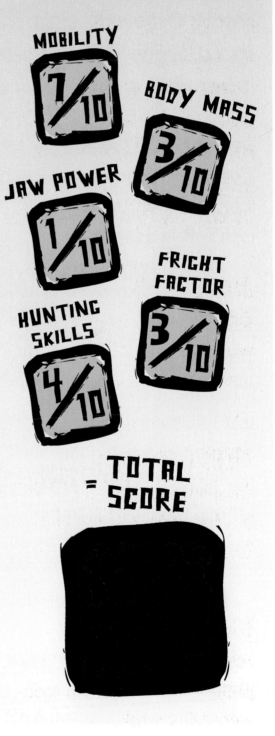

This dinosaur just manages to get into our top ten because of its high score for mobility.

MOBILITY
7/10

BODY MASS
3/10

JAW POWER
1/10

FRIGHT FACTOR
3/10

HUNTING SKILLS
4/10

= TOTAL SCORE

VELOCIRAPTOR

Velociraptor lived in Asia towards the end of the **Cretaceous** period. The first remains of this dinosaur were discovered in Mongolia by Henry Osborn in 1924. Velociraptor had a winning combination of speed, aggression and fearsome weapons – only its small size prevents it from being the overall winner. It was the size of a small turkey!

BODY MASS

An average Velociraptor would have been about 1.5 metres long, and just a metre tall at the hip. This dinosaur would have weighed about 20-25 kilograms.

JAW POWER

It had about 80 teeth that were designed for ripping and tearing flesh. Narrow **jaws** allowed Velociraptor to push its head inside the **carcass** of a dinosaur.

MOBILITY

Velociraptor was a fast-running **bipedal** dinosaur, capable of reaching speeds of 40 mph. Its name means "speedy thief."

About 12 Velociraptor fossils have been found so far. One is thought to have died whilst fighting a Protoceratops.

Velociraptor (above right) was one of the fastest and fiercest **predators** that ever lived.

FRIGHT FACTOR

Velociraptor was not much larger than a pet cat, but you would not want to meet a pack of these vicious little dinosaurs.

HUNTING SKILLS

Velociraptor was a pack hunter and a highly efficient **predator**. It attacked with the claws of all four limbs, and could even jump up onto the back of its **prey**.

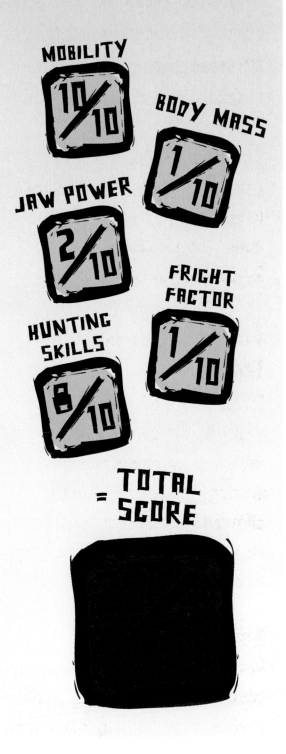

EXTREME SCORES

Too small to be more highly rated on an individual basis, but a pack of them would be a different matter.

MOBILITY 10/10

BODY MASS 1/10

JAW POWER 2/10

FRIGHT FACTOR 1/10

HUNTING SKILLS 8/10

= **TOTAL SCORE**

GIGANTOSAURUS

Palaentologists believe that **Gigantosaurus** is the largest **carnivore** that ever walked the Earth. It is also one of the most mysterious of the meat-eating dinosaurs because it was not discovered until 1994. An amateur fossil-hunter named **Ruben Carolini**, made the discovery in **Argentina** in **South America**.

BODY MASS

Gigantosaurus is the largest flesh-eating dinosaur so far discovered. It was 16 metres long and weighed about 8,000 kilograms.

JAW POWER

The jaws were crammed with narrow, pointed teeth that had serrated edges for slicing through flesh. The biggest teeth were about 20 centimetres long.

MOBILITY

For such a large animal, Gigantosaurus could run surprisingly quickly at up to 15 mph. Its slim, pointed tail may have provided balance and quick turning whilst running.

A huge – 1.8-metre long – skull housed a very small brain.

Too slow and too clumsy to be a serious contender.

FRIGHT FACTOR

Gigantosaurus was huge – bigger than Tyrannosaurus Rex – and looked very scary, but fortunately it seems to have been quite a rare dinosaur.

HUNTING SKILLS

Gigantosaurus hunted by charging at its prey with its jaws wide open. It attacked plant-eating dinosaurs that were more than 20 metres in length.

Gigantosaurus (shown here left and right) were capable of attacking and killing even large dinosaurs.

MOBILITY
1/10

BODY MASS
10/10

JAW POWER
5/10

FRIGHT FACTOR
6/10

HUNTING SKILLS
1/10

= TOTAL SCORE

TROODON

Troodon was a small **bipedal** dinosaur that lived at the very end of the **Cretaceous** period. In terms of brain-size to body weight, it may have been the brainiest animal on Earth at that time. The first Troodon **fossil** was discovered by Ferdinand V. Hayden in 1855. The US **palaeontologist** Joseph Leidy named the species in 1856.

BODY MASS

Troodon was about 2-3 metres long and weighed 40-50 kilograms. It would probably have been covered in feathers.

JAW POWER

This dinosaur had up to 100 curved teeth packed into its mouth. Each tooth had a wide, **serrated** edge for slicing through flesh.

MOBILITY

Long legs and light body weight allowed Troodon to take very big strides, so it could run extremely quickly – possibly faster than any other dinosaur.

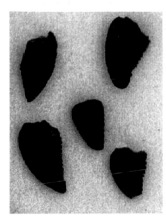

These curving teeth are responsible for the name Troodon, which means "wounding tooth".

In terms of overall body-shape, Troodon was very similar to a present-day ostrich.

FRIGHT FACTOR

It was too small to be very scary during the day, but it would be a different matter if Troodon took you by surprise in dim light.

HUNTING SKILLS

Large, forward-facing eyes suggest to scientists that Troodon may have hunted small-mammals in low-light conditions, either at night or at dawn and dusk.

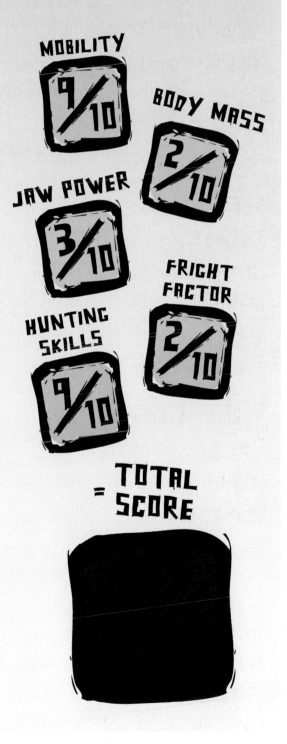

Very fast, but a lightweight dinosaur that was only really scary at night.

MOBILITY 9/10

BODY MASS 2/10

JAW POWER 3/10

FRIGHT FACTOR 2/10

HUNTING SKILLS 9/10

= TOTAL SCORE

CARCHARODONTOSAURUS

During the middle part of the **Cretaceous** period, this dinosaur was the top **predator** in North Africa. It had razor-sharp teeth, and it was big enough to attack and kill the largest plant-eating dinosaurs. German **palaeontologists** discovered Carcharodontosaurus in Morocco in 1925. Unfortunately, **fossils** of the dinosaur were destroyed during World War II.

BODY MASS

Carcharodontosaurus grew up to 15 metres in length – nearly as big as Gigantosaurus – and weighed more than 7,000 kilograms.

JAW POWER

This dinosaur had wide, powerful **jaws** the size of a human, with sharp teeth that could easily penetrate the toughest skin.

MOBILITY

Carcharodontosaurus was **bipedal**, but it relied on power and weight rather than speed and it could not run very quickly.

FRIGHT FACTOR

This dinosaur was big and very fierce, but it was also quite slow moving, so you could probably manage to run away if it spotted you.

A fragment of the dinosaur's skull and upper jaw.

The appearance of Carcharodontosaurus has been reconstructed from just a few fossil bones.

Low scores for speed and hunting are responsible for this giant killer not being more highly rated.

MOBILITY
2/10

BODY MASS
9/10

JAW POWER
4/10

FRIGHT FACTOR
9/10

HUNTING SKILLS
2/10

= TOTAL SCORE

HUNTING SKILLS

Carcharodontosaurus was probably an ambush hunter that waited in hiding until it could launch a surprise attack.

Albertosaurus was a sleek, saw-toothed **predator** that hunted **Hadrosaurs** and other plant-eating dinosaurs. It lived in North America during the last part of the **Cretaceous** period. Geologist Joseph Tyrell discovered **fossils** of Albertosaurus in 1884 in Alberta, Canada.

BODY MASS

Albertosaurus measured more than 8 metres in length, stood 4 metres high at the hip and weighed about 3,000 kilograms.

JAW POWER

Albertosaurus had a big head, with large, powerful **jaws**. There were about 36 razor-sharp teeth in its upper jaw, and about 30 in the lower jaw.

MOBILITY

This large **bipedal** dinosaur may have reached 19 mph when running at top speed, as fast as any other dinosaur of its size.

FRIGHT FACTOR

This was a very scary dinosaur because it combined large size with fast speed, which made it a deadly hunter.

This skull still has most of the teeth intact.

This was a big, fast predator, but there were other dinosaurs that were bigger and faster.

HUNTING SKILLS

Albertosaurus may not have been a very good hunter, because its eyes are positioned at the side of its head. Predators see better when their eyes are at the front.

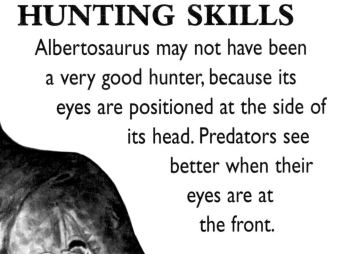

MOBILITY
6/10

BODY MASS
5/10

JAW POWER
8/10

FRIGHT FACTOR
4/10

HUNTING SKILLS
5/10

= TOTAL SCORE

Like other bipedal dinosaurs, Albertosaurus used its tail for balance.

ALLOSAURUS

Allosaurus was once the largest **predator** on Earth. It lived at the end of the **Jurassic** period and the beginning of the **Cretaceous** period. The first **fossils** were discovered in 1879 in Wyoming, USA, by the famous fossil-hunter Othniel C. Marsh.

BODY MASS

Allosaurus was about 12 metres long when fully grown. This giant also weighed more than 4,000 kilograms.

JAW POWER

Allosaurus had about 70 sharp teeth, and each tooth was up to 10 centimetres long. But the teeth were fragile, and broke off easily.

Allosaurus was capable of killing even the biggest plant-eating dinosaurs.

Allosaurus was a top predator with no natural enemies.

EXTREME SCORES

A serious contender for the number one spot – but its slow speed and lack of stamina reduce its overall scariness.

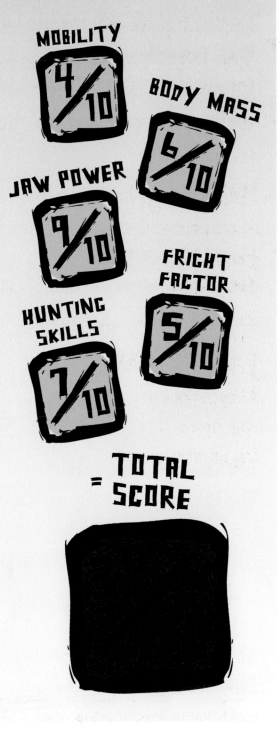

MOBILITY
4/10

BODY MASS
6/10

JAW POWER
9/10

FRIGHT FACTOR
5/10

HUNTING SKILLS
7/10

= **TOTAL SCORE**

MOBILITY

This **bipedal** carnivore may have had a top speed of about 12 mph, but it had no **stamina** for a long chase.

FRIGHT FACTOR

This dinosaur was even bigger and more aggressive than Albertosaurus – just hope that it gets tired before you do!

HUNTING SKILLS

Allosaurus may have hunted in packs, using the 15-centimetre claws on its forelimbs to slash open its prey.

19

SPINOSAURUS

Spinosaurus was a fierce **predator** that lived in Africa during the mid **Cretaceous** period. It had a strange 2-metre tall crest along its back that was made of long spines covered by tough skin. The first fossil of Spinosaurus was discovered in Egypt in 1912 by German **palaeontologist** Ernst Stromer von Reichenbach.

BODY MASS

Spinosaurus reached lengths of up to 15 metres, and weighed up to 7,000 kilograms.

JAW POWER

This dinosaur had long, narrow jaws lined with razor sharp, pointed teeth.

MOBILITY

The longer than usual forelimbs suggest that Spinosaurus may have walked on all fours at least some of the time.

Spinosaurus looked as strange as any fairy tale dragon, but it was a real animal.

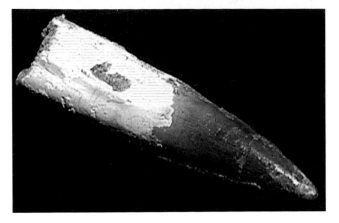

Each tooth was designed to penetrate deeply into a **prey's** flesh.

HUNTING SKILLS

The design of the jaws and teeth suggest that Spinosaurus probably fed mainly on fish that it snatched from rivers and lakes.

FRIGHT FACTOR

This dinosaur is straight out of your worst nightmares – a gigantic heavyweight killer with jaws like a crocodile.

Spinosaurus was large and fierce – for a fish-eater – but a bit too slow to score any higher.

MOBILITY
5/10

BODY MASS
7/10

JAW POWER
6/10

FRIGHT FACTOR
8/10

HUNTING SKILLS
6/10

= TOTAL SCORE
32/50

TYRANNOSAURUS REX

This is the most famous of all the dinosaurs and one of the biggest land **predators** that has ever lived. It is often known as Tyrannosaurus Rex (or T Rex), because "rex" means "king" in the **Latin** language. The first **fossils** were discovered in 1908 in Montana, USA, by fossil-hunter Barnum Brown.

BODY MASS

Tyrannosaurus was 12 metres long and weighed more than 7,000 kilograms, but it had very puny little forelimbs that only grew to about 1 metre.

MOBILITY

This **bipedal carnivore** could run at speeds of up to 18 mph, but only over short distances.

This killer could tear off 200 kilograms of flesh with a single bite.

JAW POWER

Tyrannosaurus had massive **jaws** with very powerful muscles, and it could bite straight through even the biggest bones.

Tyrannosaurus was part of a family of dinosaurs called Tyrannosaurids. Above are three more types.

This massive and terrifying killer had huge jaws and hind limbs, but its forelimbs were definitely undersized.

MOBILITY
3/10

BODY MASS
8/10

JAW POWER
10/10

FRIGHT FACTOR
10/10

HUNTING SKILLS
3/10

= TOTAL SCORE

FRIGHT FACTOR

The sight of this monster charging at you would probably frighten you to death.

HUNTING SKILLS

Tyrannosaurus probably stalked herds of plant-eating dinosaurs and picked off the weakest members – the very young and the very old.

Deinonychus was the supreme dinosaur **predator** – a fast and deadly pack hunter. It lived in **North America** during the early part of the **Cretaceous** period. Deinonychus was discovered in 1931 in Montana, USA, by **fossil** hunter Barnum Brown, and was named in 1964 by US **palaeontologist** John Ostrom.

BODY MASS

Deinonychus was a medium-sized **carnivore** that weighed about 80 kilograms and stood 2 metres tall.

JAW POWER

A combination of powerful **jaw** muscles and curved teeth with **serrated** edges meant that Deinonychus could bite off huge chunks of flesh.

MOBILITY

Deinonychus was a fast-running, **agile** predator that could attack with the claws of all four limbs as well as its teeth.

Each tooth could cut through skin and muscle like the blade of a knife.

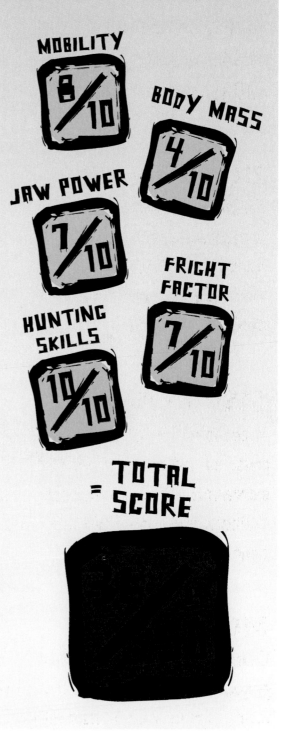

The fastest, fiercest, and most fearsome – this dinosaur is enough to give even a Tyrannosaurus bad dreams.

MOBILITY
8/10

BODY MASS
4/10

JAW POWER
7/10

FRIGHT FACTOR
7/10

HUNTING SKILLS
10/10

= TOTAL SCORE

FRIGHT FACTOR

Just one of these dinosaurs was scary, and no animal stood a chance against a whole pack of these vicious killers.

Although Deinonychus was no taller than a human being, it carried an incredible amount of killing power.

HUNTING SKILLS

Its hind limbs were equipped with long, vicious claws that were capable of hanging onto and ripping open the flesh of the largest prey.

Before deciding our Top Ten Dinosaurs, we also considered these animals – all of them were deadly killers, but not quite deadly enough to make the Top Ten.

HERRERASAURUS

Herrerasaurus was one of the very first meat-eating **theropod** dinosaurs. It lived in South America about 225 million years ago during the **Triassic** period. Herrerasaurus was about three metres long and weighed about 200 kilograms. It walked and ran on its hind legs, and would have hunted small and medium-sized plant-eating dinosaurs, such as Pisanosaurus.

COELOPHYSIS

Coelophysis was a vicious pack-hunter that lived in North America during the late Triassic period. This small theropod dinosaur was about 3 metres long, but weighed just 25 kilograms. Hundreds of Coelophysis **fossils** were discovered at Ghost Ranch in New Mexico, USA, in the 1940s. Analysis of the fossils revealed that Coelophysis was a cannibal that sometimes ate its own kind.

BARYONYX

Baryonyx was a slightly smaller relative of Spinosaurus that lived in Europe and Africa about 120 million years ago. It measured about 10 metres in length and weighed about 2,000 kilograms. Like its larger relative, Baryonyx was a **bipedal** dinosaur that probably specialized in hunting fish, snatching them out of the water with its long jaws.

COMPSOGNATHUS

Compsognathus was one of the smallest known dinosaurs. It measured just 90 centimetres long and most of the length was in the tail. That did not stop it from being an **agile** and efficient **predator**. This tiny theropod was only about the size of a chicken and lived during the middle of the Jurassic period. Compsognathus was bipedal, and used the claws on its forefeet to hold its prey while it bit off chunks of flesh.

STRUTHIOMIMUS

This fast, bipedal omnivore lived in North America about 75 million years ago. Its name means "ostrich mimic" and like the present-day ostrich, this theropod dinosaur ate anything that it could find. Struthiomimus had large eyes at the sides of its head, and was constantly on the alert for danger. When threatened by larger predators, Struthiomimus could run away at speeds of up to 40 mph.

NO. 10 DILOPHOSAURUS

		Extreme Scores	
Dinosaur type	Theropod	**Body mass**	3
Fossil location	North America	**Mobility**	7
Size	6 m	**Jaw power**	1
Lived when	190 million years ago	**Hunting skills**	4
Discovered by	Samuel Welles	**Fright factor**	3
Notable feature	Head crest		

TOTAL SCORE 18/50

NO. 9 VELOCIRAPTOR

		Extreme Scores	
Dinosaur type	Theropod	**Body mass**	1
Fossil location	Asia	**Mobility**	10
Size	60 cm	**Jaw power**	2
Lived when	70 million years ago	**Hunting skills**	8
Discovered by	Henry Osborn	**Fright factor**	1
Notable feature	80 teeth		

TOTAL SCORE 22/50

NO. 8 GIGANTOSAURUS

		Extreme Scores	
Dinosaur type	Theropod	**Body mass**	10
Fossil location	South America	**Mobility**	1
Size	16 m	**Jaw power**	5
Lived when	110 million years ago	**Hunting skills**	1
Discovered by	Ruben Carolini	**Fright factor**	6
Notable feature	2 metre skull		

TOTAL SCORE 23/50

NO. 7 TROODON

		Extreme Scores	
Dinosaur type	Theropod	**Body mass**	2
Fossil location	North America	**Mobility**	9
Size	2 m	**Jaw power**	3
Lived when	65 million years ago	**Hunting skills**	9
Discovered by	Joseph Leidy	**Fright factor**	2
Notable feature	Intelligence		

TOTAL SCORE 25/50

NO. 6 CARCHARODONTOSAURUS

		Extreme Scores	
Dinosaur type	Theropod	**Body mass**	9
Fossil location	Africa	**Mobility**	2
Size	15 m	**Jaw power**	4
Lived when	100 million years ago	**Hunting skills**	2
Discovered by	Dr Stromer	**Fright factor**	9
Notable feature	2 metre jaws		

TOTAL SCORE 26/50

NO. 5 ALBERTOSAURUS

Dinosaur type	Theropod	Extreme Scores		
Fossil location	North America	Body mass		5
Size	8 m	Mobility		6
Lived when	75 million years ago	Jaw power		8
Discovered by	Joseph Tyrell	Hunting skills		5
Notable Feature	Bulk and speed	Fright factor		4

TOTAL SCORE 28/50

NO. 4 ALLOSAURUS

Dinosaur type	Theropod	Extreme Scores		
Fossil location	North America	Body mass		6
Size	12 m	Mobility		4
Lived when	150 million years ago	Jaw power		9
Discovered by	Othniel C Marsh	Hunting skills		7
Notable Feature	Aggression	Fright factor		5

TOTAL SCORE 31/50

NO. 3 SPINOSAURUS

Dinosaur type	Theropod	Extreme Scores		
Fossil location	Africa	Body mass		7
Size	15 m	Mobility		5
Lived when	80 million years ago	Jaw power		6
Discovered by	Ernst Stromer	Hunting skills		6
Notable Feature	Long jaws	Fright factor		8

TOTAL SCORE 32/50

NO. 2 TYRANNOSAURUS REX

Dinosaur type	Theropod	Extreme Scores		
Fossil location	North America	Body mass		8
Size	12 m	Mobility		3
Lived when	65 million years ago	Jaw power		10
Discovered by	Barnum Brown	Hunting skills		3
Notable Feature	Jaw muscles	Fright factor		10

TOTAL SCORE 34/50

NO. 1 DEINONYCHUS

Dinosaur type	Theropod	Extreme Scores		
Fossil location	North America	Body mass		4
Size	2 m	Mobility		8
Lived when	100 million years ago	Jaw power		7
Discovered by	Barnum Brown	Hunting skills		10
Notable Feature	Ripping claws	Fright factor		7

TOTAL SCORE 36/50

AGILE something that can move quickly and easily

BIPEDAL a two-footed animal

CARCASS the dead body of an animal

CARNIVORE a meat-eating animal

CARRION the dead and rotting body of an animal

CREST a tuft or ridge on the head of a bird or other animal

CRETACEOUS the last period before the extinction of the dinosaurs – 146 to 65 million years ago

DINOSAUR land-living reptiles that lived during the Triassic, Jurassic and Cretaceous periods

FOSSIL the remains of a dead animal that has turned to stone

HADROSAUR group of large bipedal dinosaurs that had a horny, duck-like bill and webbed feet

JAWS the structures that form the framework of the mouth and hold the teeth

JURASSIC the middle period when dinosaurs were a dominant species – 208 to 146 million years ago

LATIN an ancient language still used by scientists to give the official name of animal species

OSTRICH large, swift-running flightless bird of Africa. It has a long bare neck, small head, and two-toed feet. It is the largest living bird

PALAEONTOLOGIST scientist who specializes in the study of fossil organisms and related remains

PREDATOR an animal that lives by preying on other animals

PREY an animal hunted or caught for food

SERRATED notched like the edge of a saw

STAMINA lasting strength and energy

THEROPOD group of carnivorous dinosaurs with short forelimbs that walked or ran on strong hind legs